Rabbit Ear Fold

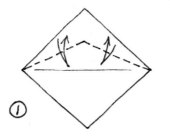

①

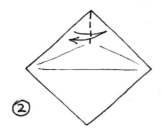

②

③

④

Squash Fold

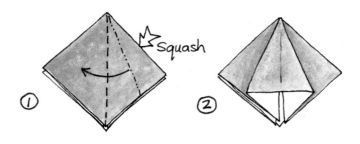

① Squash

②

Petal Fold

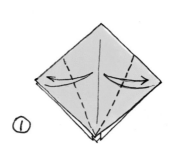

①

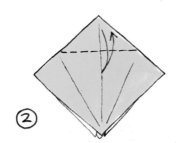

②

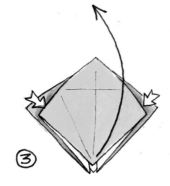

③

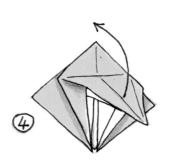

④

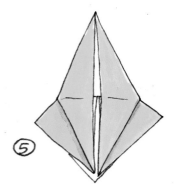

⑤

Kite Base

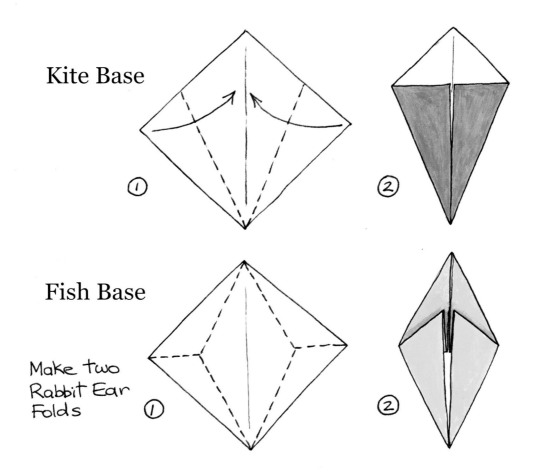

① ②

Fish Base

Make two
Rabbit Ear
Folds

① ②

Big Blue Groper (Fish Base)

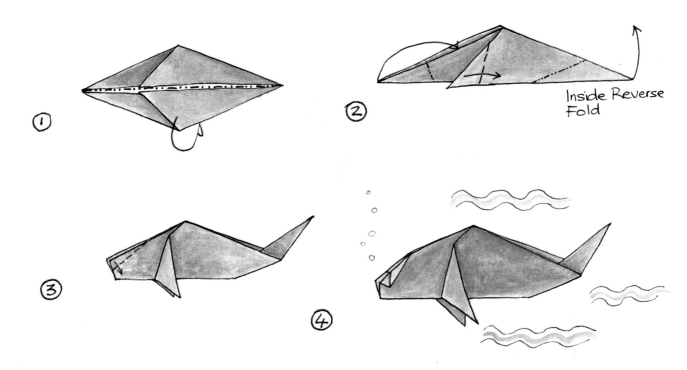

① ② Inside Reverse
Fold

③ ④

Little Penguin
(Kite Base)

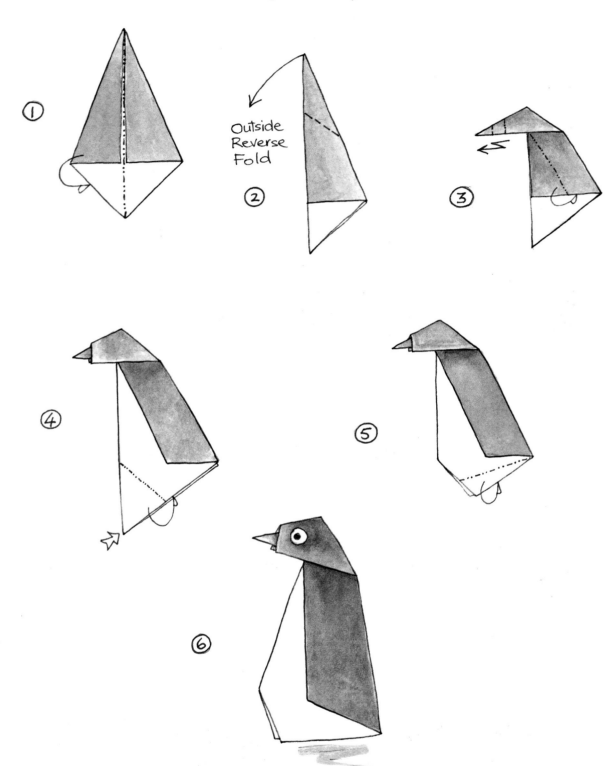

①

② Outside Reverse Fold

③

④

⑤

⑥

Swan
(Kite Base)

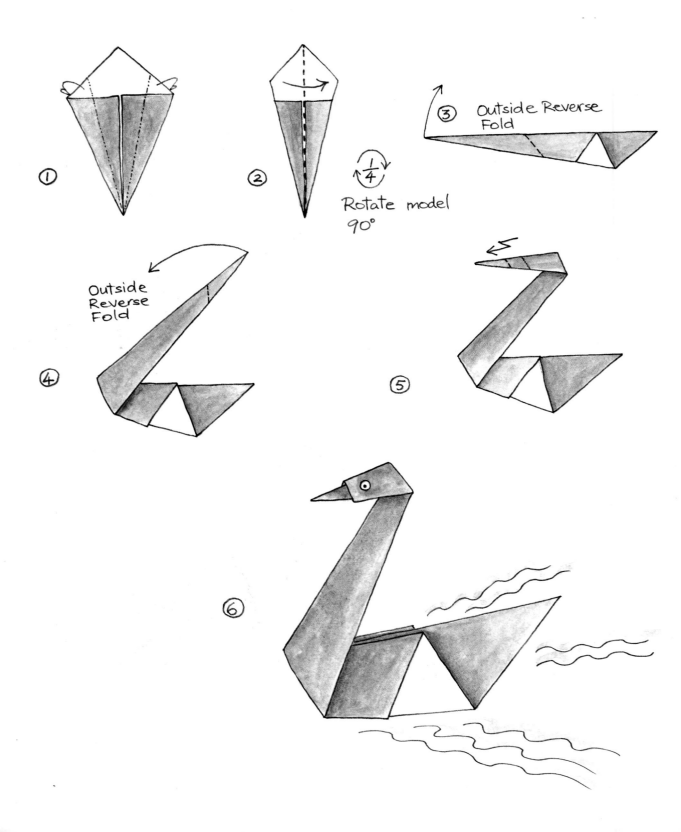

①

②

$\frac{1}{4}$ Rotate model 90°

③ Outside Reverse Fold

④ Outside Reverse Fold

⑤

⑥

Australian Fur Seal
(Fish Base)

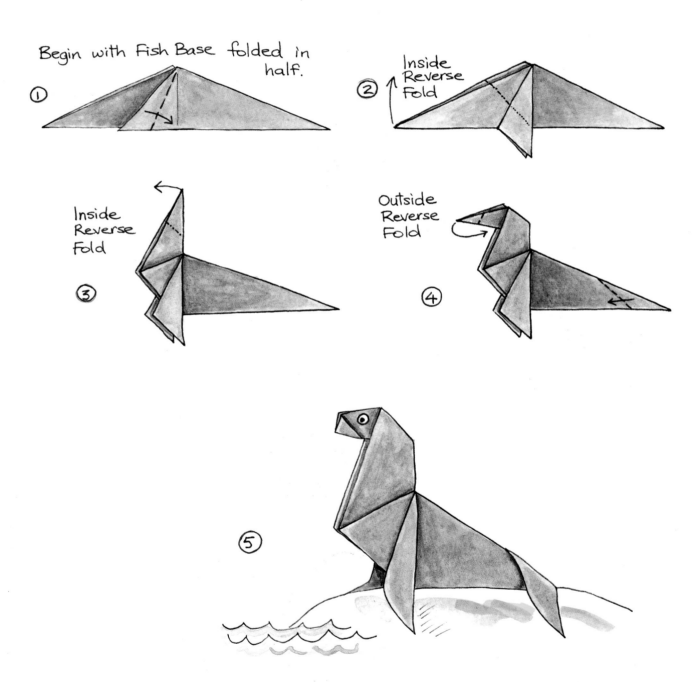

Begin with Fish Base folded in half.

①

② Inside Reverse Fold

③ Inside Reverse Fold

④ Outside Reverse Fold

⑤

Black-headed Honeyeater

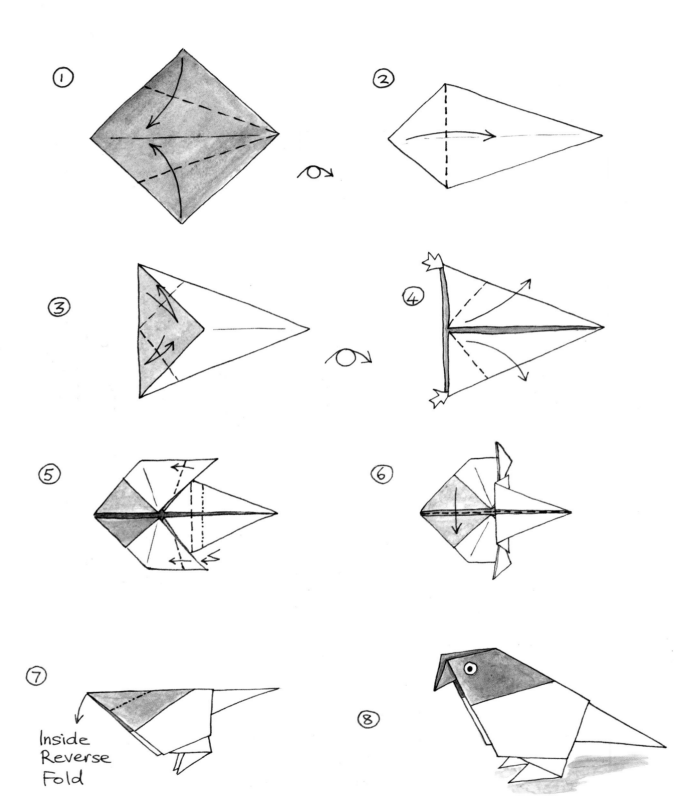

Inside
Reverse
Fold

Seven-Spotted Ladybird

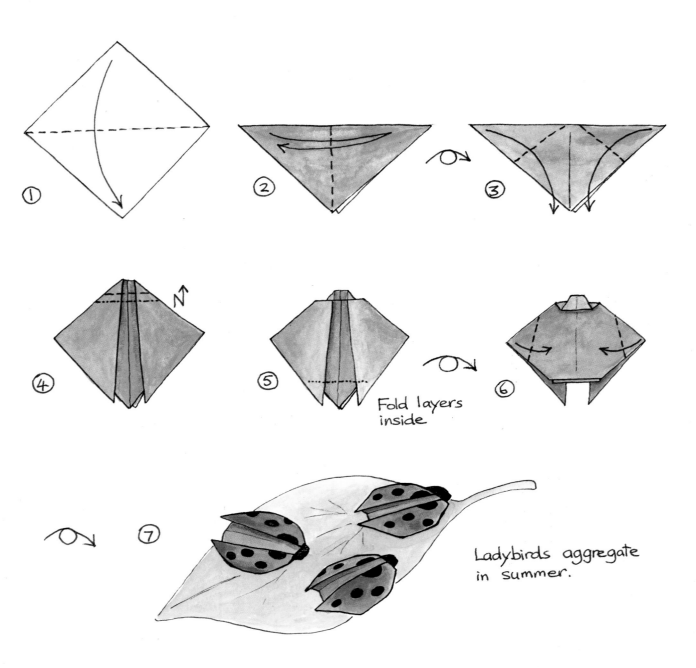

① ② ③

④ ⑤ Fold layers inside ⑥

⑦

Ladybirds aggregate in summer.

Riddle
A toad, a seal, a smart black crow,
Koala with his mum below,
A beetle red, a turtle green,
And the elusive Thylacine.
All these creatures (some are fat),
Made up of something rather flat.

Possum

①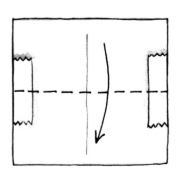

Reinforce edges with tape.

②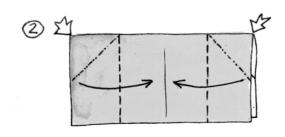

③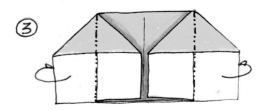

④

⑤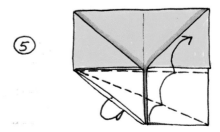

⑥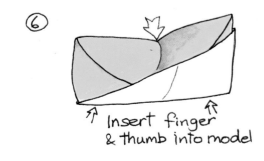

Insert finger & thumb into model

⑦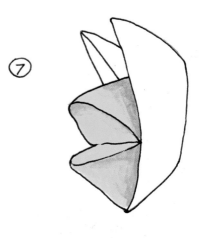

⑧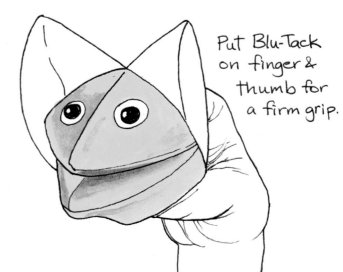

Put Blu-Tack on finger & thumb for a firm grip.

Tasmanian Devil pup

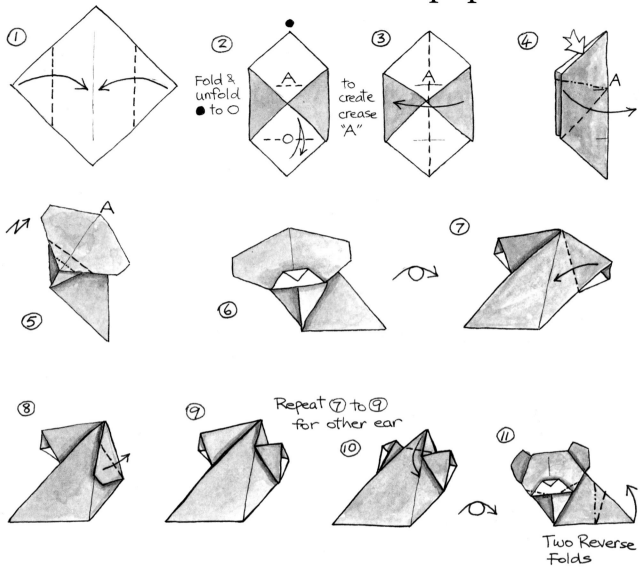

①

② Fold & unfold ● to ○

to create crease "A"

③

④

⑤

⑥

⑦

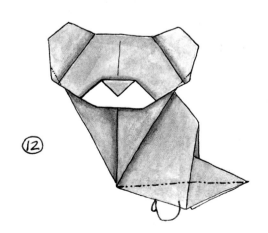

⑧

⑨

Repeat ⑦ to ⑨ for other ear

⑩

⑪ Two Reverse Folds

⑫

⑬

Frog Base

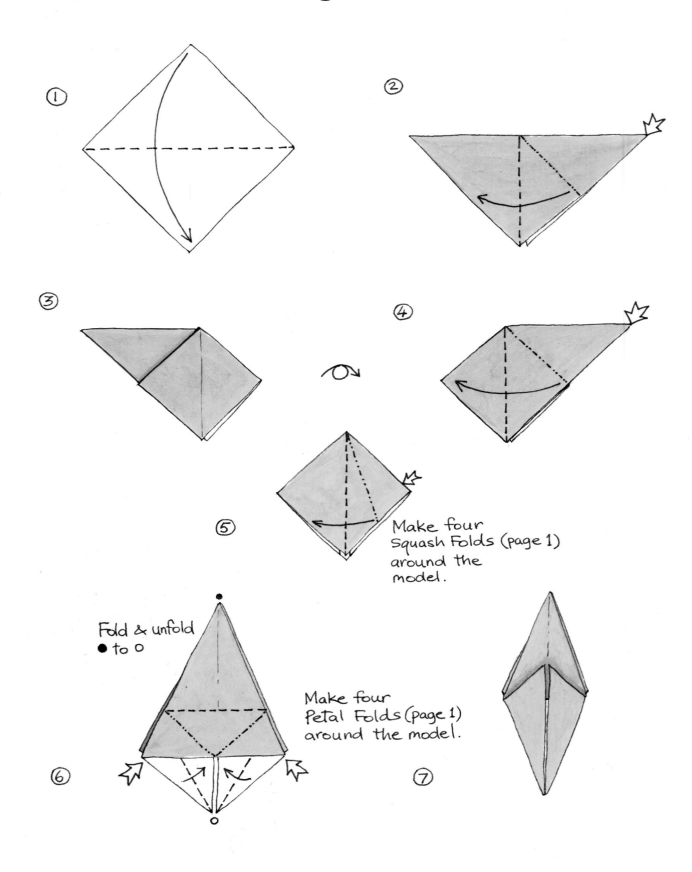

① ②

③ ④

⑤ Make four
Squash Folds (page 1)
around the
model.

Fold & unfold
● to ○

Make four
Petal Folds (page 1)
around the model.

⑥ ⑦

Green Tree Frog

①

② Repeat for other three faces of model

③

④ Inside Reverse Fold

⑤ Inside Reverse Fold

⑥ Inside Reverse Fold

⑦ Inside Reverse Folds

⑧ Blow

Inside Reverse Fold

⑨

Koala

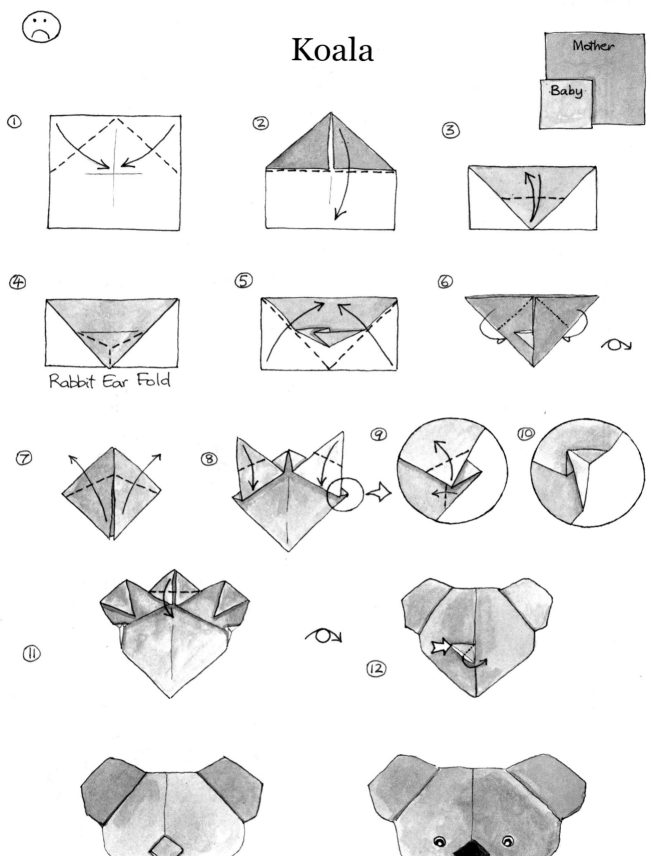

Mother

Baby

① ② ③

④ Rabbit Ear Fold ⑤ ⑥

⑦ ⑧ ⑨ ⑩

⑪ ⑫

⑬ ⑭

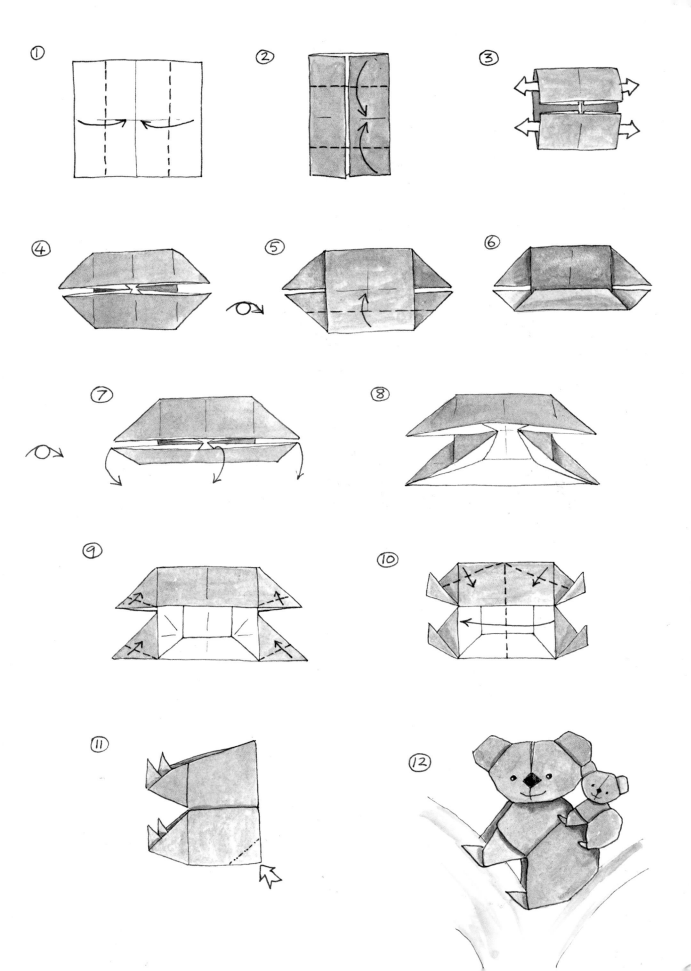

Wombat

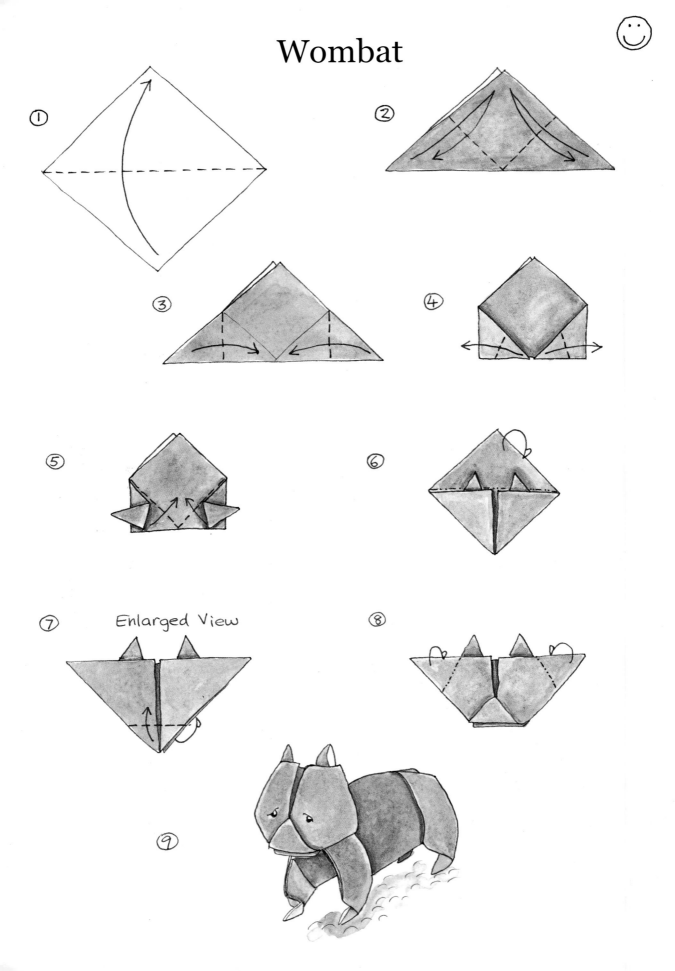

⑦ Enlarged View

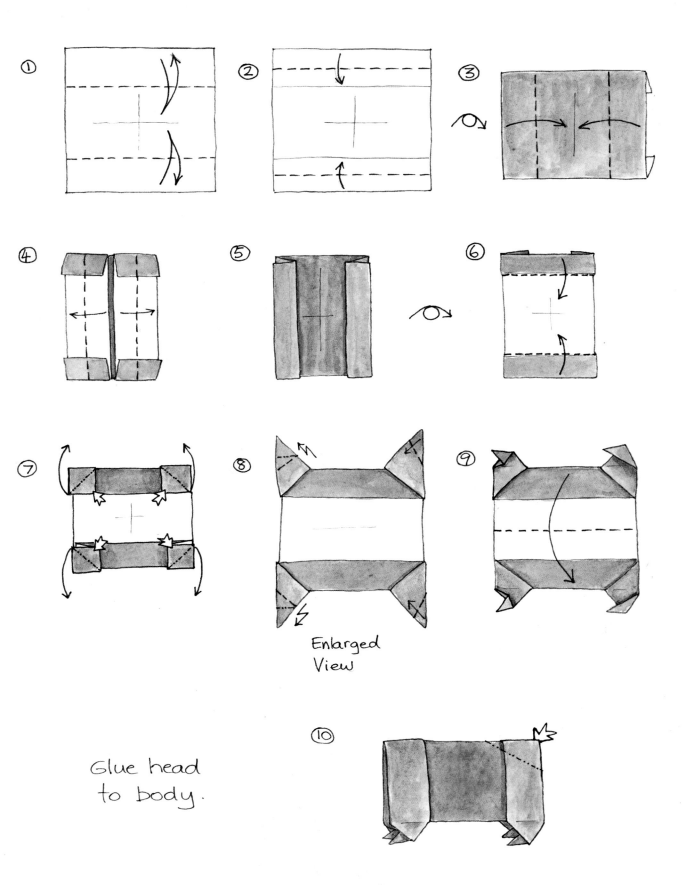

① ② ③

④ ⑤ ⑥

⑦ ⑧ Enlarged View ⑨

Glue head to body.

⑩

Bird Base

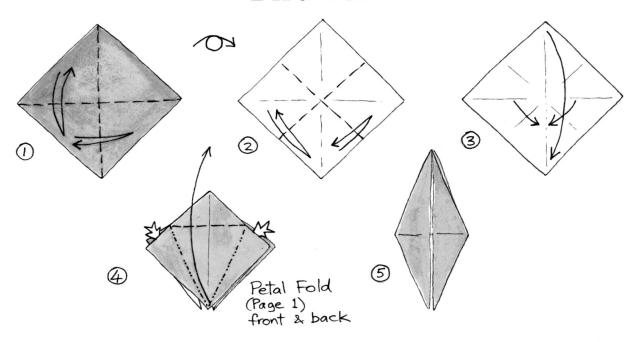

① ② ③

④ Petal Fold
(Page 1)
front & back

⑤

Emu (Bird Base)
Large paper recommended

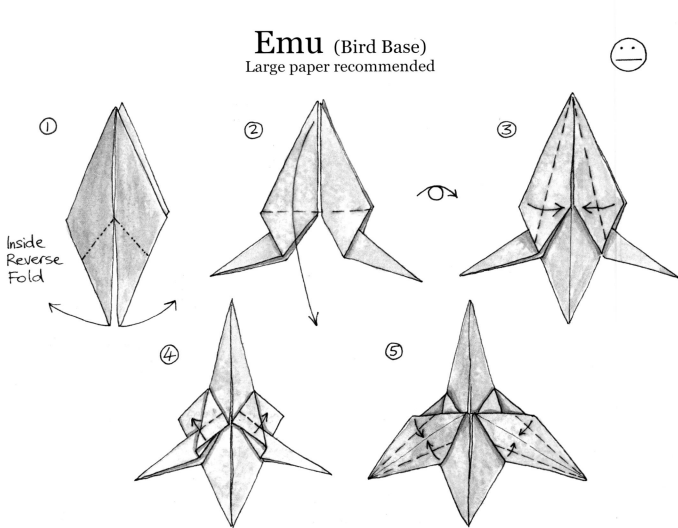

① Inside
Reverse
Fold

②

③

④

⑤

Emu (continued)

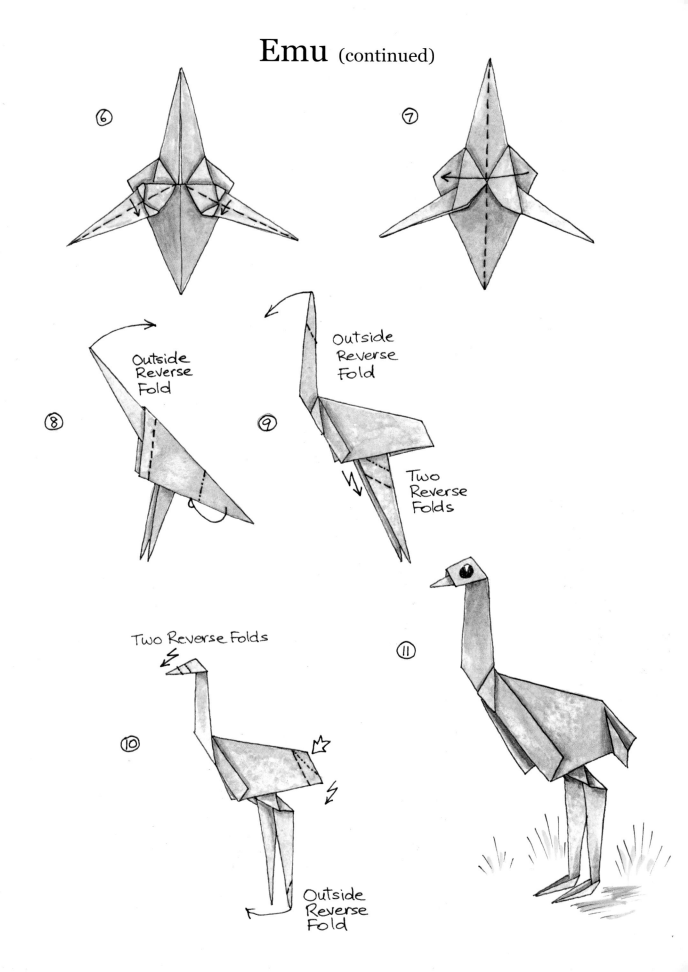

⑥

⑦

⑧ Outside Reverse Fold

⑨ Outside Reverse Fold

Two Reverse Folds

⑩ Two Reverse Folds

Outside Reverse Fold

⑪

Cane Toad

①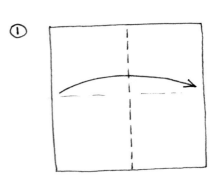

②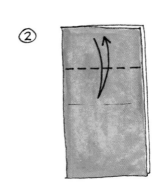

③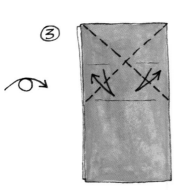

④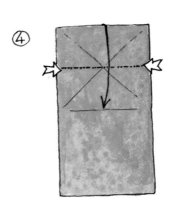

⑤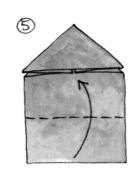

⑥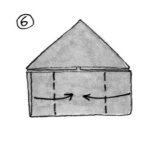

⑦

⑧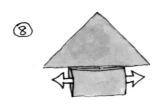

⑨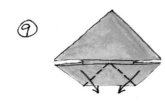

⑩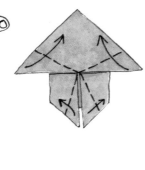

⑪

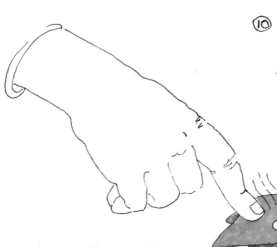

⑫

Australian Crow
(upside down Bird Base)

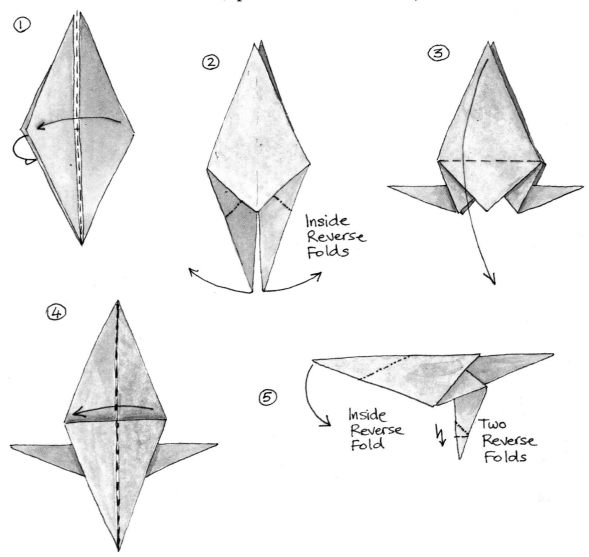

①

② Inside Reverse Folds

③

④

⑤ Inside Reverse Fold   Two Reverse Folds

Aussie Crows
have learned how to roll
Cane Toads onto their backs
to eat them, avoiding their
poisonous glands.

⑥

Thylacine (2 Bird Bases)

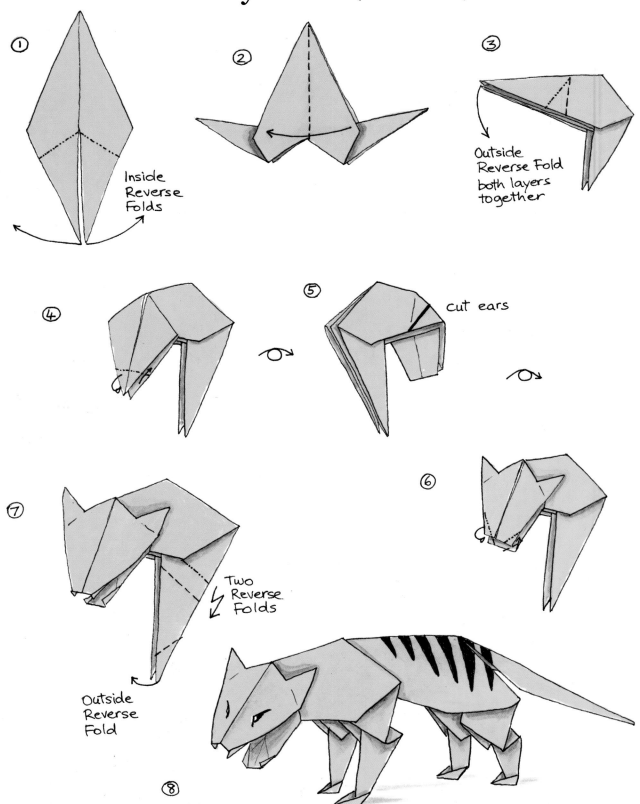

① Inside Reverse Folds

②

③ Outside Reverse Fold both layers together

④

⑤ cut ears

⑥

⑦ Two Reverse Folds

Outside Reverse Fold

⑧

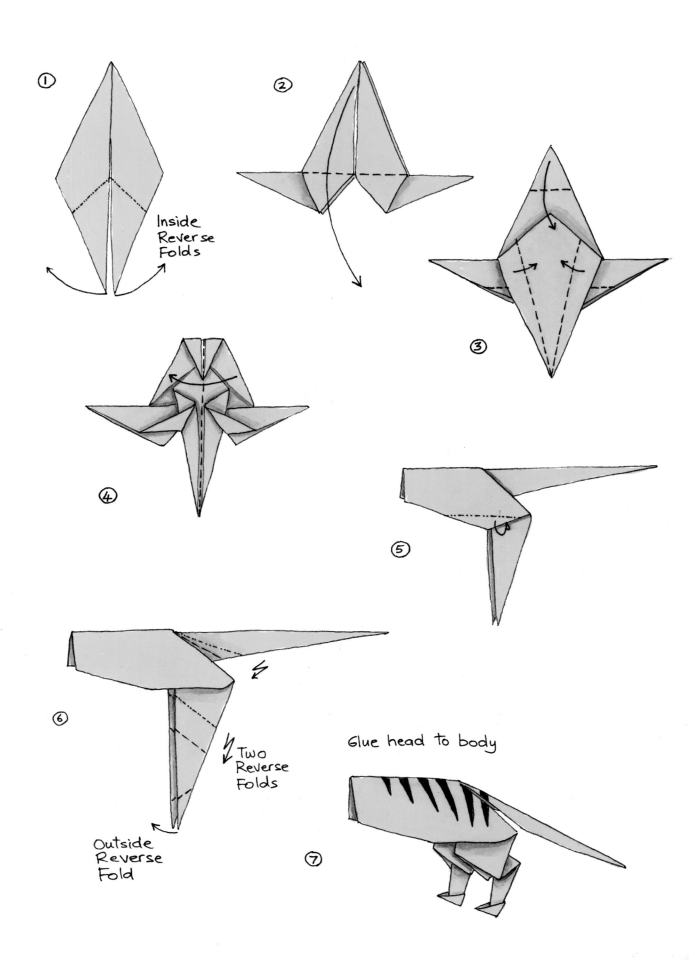

① Inside Reverse Folds

②

③

④

⑤

⑥ Two Reverse Folds

Outside Reverse Fold

Glue head to body

⑦

Kangaroo (Bird Base)
large paper recommended

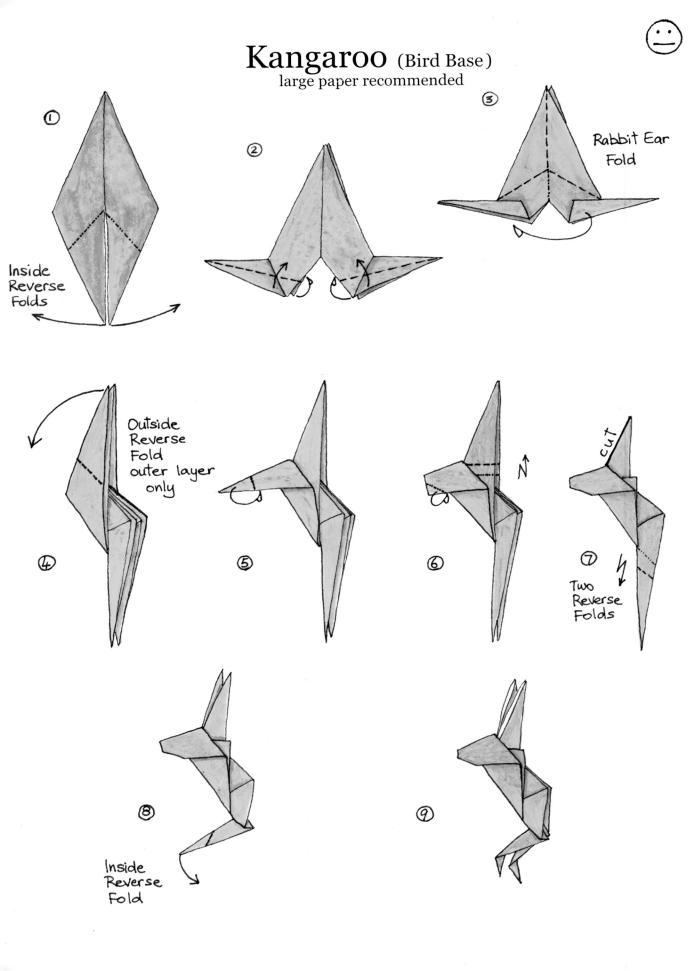

① Inside Reverse Folds

②

③ Rabbit Ear Fold

④ Outside Reverse Fold outer layer only

⑤

⑥

⑦ cut — Two Reverse Folds

⑧ Inside Reverse Fold

⑨

Fold as for Thylacine body up to step 5.

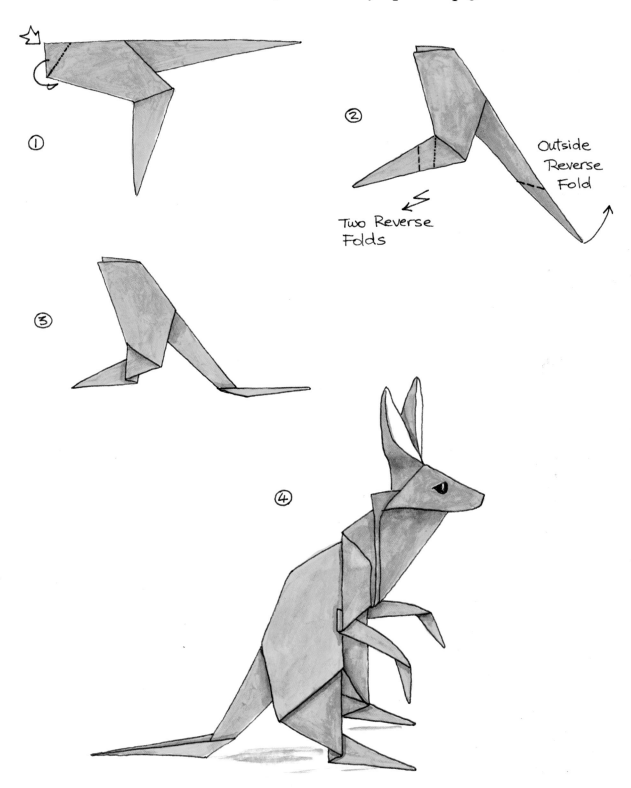

①

②

Two Reverse Folds

Outside Reverse Fold

③

④

Flatback Turtle
(upside down Bird Base)

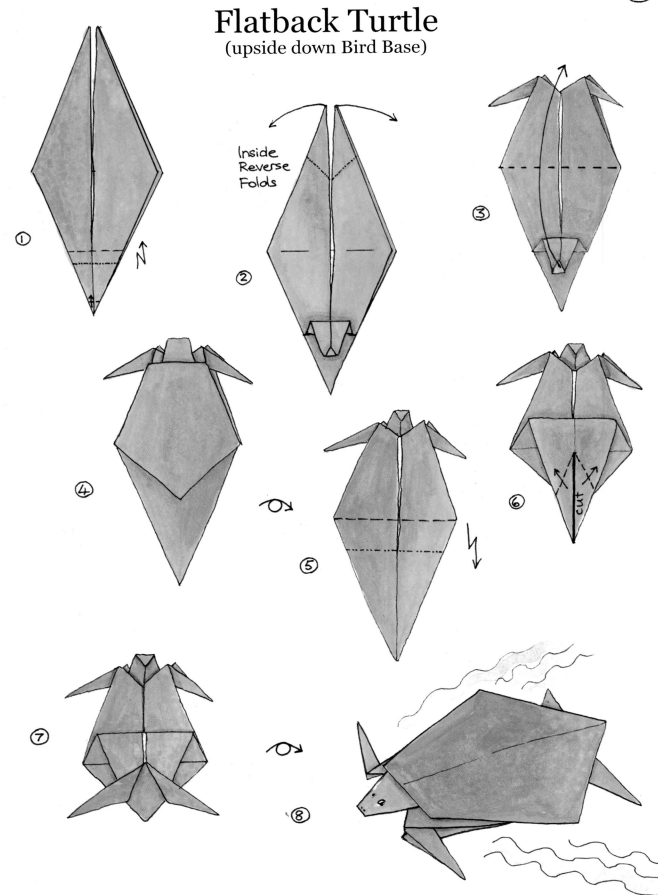

Inside Reverse Folds

cut